Golden Threads

Geoff Woodcock

onewithchrist.org

Thanks to Brian Upsher for editorial support, Nikki Miller and Claire Latta for proofing. And of course, thanks to my wife Melanie, without whom this book would not have been possible.

Golden Threads by Geoff Woodcock

ISBN: 978-1-991387-38-7

Published by Acacia Media | www.acacia.media

Printed in the United States of America

Other Formats

978-1-991387-41-7 (PDF)

978-1-991387-40-0 (Kindle)

978-1-991387-39-4 (ePub)

This book is available free online at www.onewithchrist.org

Visit https://mariakemp.art for Golden Threads cover art prints.

Contents

Foreword

John 15:11 (NLT)
"I have told you these things so that you will be filled with my joy.
Yes, your joy will overflow!"

God has a vision for your life and it is breathtaking. It is not only about what you can do, but about who you can become in Christ, and it is revealed through almost every promise of Scripture. The Bible says that Jesus wants to heal your heart and fill you to overflowing with His joy.[1] He longs to lift your burdens and wash all your stress away in a river of His peace.[2] Jesus wants to erase your sin and remove it from you as far as the east is from the west, not just so you can enjoy being forgiven, but so you can be truly free.[3] And in the place of your sin, Jesus wants to turn your heart into a channel of a love that never wavers and never ends, a love that He says stretches from eternity to eternity.[4] This is His vision for your life, and He is inviting you to share it. He won't force it upon you, so in keeping with the way of grace, you are free to take it or leave it. It's up to you.

No one would blame you for rejecting it. After all, while the theory may sound good, who on earth really believes it? Who is convinced that the blood of Jesus erases their sin out of all existence? For most of us, the memories of our past failures are too vivid for us to take hold of the innocence that Christ offers. And who is there that dares to pursue the fullness of joy in a world of such pain and suffering? And who truly believes that God's love for us is both infinite and eternal? Our daily experience seems so far removed from this vision of love that it is far easier not to believe. We hear the call of God's love, but all around us, we see so much failure. Even in the Scriptures we read of so many people who doubted God,

i

denied His promises, and went back to what they knew. Why should we be any different?

Psalm 81:10-11
"I am the LORD your God, who brought you out of the land of Egypt; Open your mouth wide, and I will fill it. But My people would not heed My voice, and Israel would have none of Me."

A long time ago, the Lord called His people to open wide their hearts that He might satisfy their hunger with His abundance. He wanted to take them into a land flowing with milk and honey, but they would have none of Him. The people of Israel turned away from a life of unknown fruitfulness to die in a familiar wilderness. In doing so, they denied God the opportunity to express the full intensity of His love. Yet after all this time, God's heart is still the same. He still wants to lavish people with His love and is looking for anyone who will receive it. *He is looking for you. Will you be different?*

Because God is eternally good, we don't have to try to convince the Father to be good to us—Scripture says that His goodness and love have been pursuing us all the days of our life.[5] We simply need to stop running. And because God is infinitely good, He must always want the absolute best for us, and that best will always stretch the limits of our imagination. For example, the Father says that He wants to pour out so much of His goodness upon us that people tremble in awe when they meet us.[6] Just imagine it! This is a vision so extreme that it can only come from God.

So here we stand, at the edge of our Promised Land. As we survey our inheritance and see the giants and anticipate the battles, we must forget all our past failures and instead prepare our hearts to overcome together. We must remember that God's promises remain true in the face of every circumstance. He knows how to make His vision our reality. Our part is simply to take His hand and follow His voice and He will do the rest.

So let's take the next step together into the life God has prepared for us.

Designed for Love

1

Before He spoke the universe into being, God had a vision in His heart, a well-defined image of what creation would look like. When He created the universe, the Father established an overarching principle of life: that everything would flourish when it lives in design. We can see this principle at work all around us. We know that when plants receive light, water and nutrients, they grow and thrive and then bless the world with their beauty. When they are denied these, they languish and die. The same principle is also true for people. We only truly flourish when we are living in our design.

So are we alive and thriving or just surviving? If we don't feel like we're fully living in God's vision for our lives, then we can start by seeking to discover His design.

Individual Design

Even before we were born, God had a plan for our lives. So let's start at the very beginning. Scripture says that God is good and does good and that is especially true of God at our creation.[7] When the Father created people, He made us as living gifts of His love for Jesus and He infused us with His life and beauty.[8] He delighted in His design for humanity, declaring that it was *very* good![9]

However, it did not take long for humanity to fall and for sin to break our hearts at the deepest level. Yet our failure did not change God's original plan for us—His design remains constant, unchangeable and attainable. And if we can rediscover our design, not only will we find the key to flourishing, but we will also find an energizing sense of meaning and purpose in life.

So what are we made for? In the natural realm, we know that every creation is made for a specific purpose. Ovens are made to heat food, clocks are built to tell the time, lamps are made to give light and so on. If we had to give one command to an invention, that command would always express its primary purpose. So, if we built an oven and gave it just one command, we would say: *cook food*. Likewise, if we gave one instruction to a clock, it would be: *tell the time*. In each case, the ultimate purpose of a creation is made known when we give it its one most important command.

The Most Important Command

Matthew 22:34-40 (NLT)
But when the Pharisees heard that he had silenced the Sadducees with his reply, they met together to question him again. One of them, an expert in religious law, tried to trap him with this question: "Teacher, which is the most important commandment in the law of Moses?"

Jesus replied, "'You must love the Lord your God with all your heart, all your soul, and all your mind.' This is the first and greatest commandment. A second is equally important: 'Love your neighbor as yourself.' The entire law and all the demands of the prophets are based on these two commandments."

God has not made the question of our design an unknowable mystery, and neither is it subject to personal interpretation. Here Jesus gives us our single most important command: to love God with our entire being. By giving us this one command, Jesus is revealing God's glorious design for our lives. Just as a clock is made to tell the time, the Father has perfectly engineered us— heart, soul, mind, and body—for a life of love. And just as a clock's sense of purpose in life would only ever be found in telling the time, so we can only find our true meaning in life as we learn to love God with all our heart and soul. This is our reason for being, and it is worthy of endless repetition: God created us for a life of love. Every single person is designed for this one thing, and it is *very* good!

Deep down, we all know we are made for love. We have been searching for love our entire lives, but we let our selfishness blind us to the reason for our creation. Many of us have been so broken for so long that we struggle to believe we could ever love God with *all* our heart. Even as a church, we have lost sight of God's vision for love. Ask yourself: when was the last time you heard a sermon on the greatest command? Why is it so tragically rare to hear teaching about the greatest, most important thing in life? Could there be anything else more important?

As the Body of Christ, we need to put the first command back into first place. Until we do, all around the world, people will continue to come to church and sit in rows of broken hearts, waiting for someone to tell them what we are made for, waiting to hear the words we all need to believe: *We are children of the God who is Love and we bear His image. God made us to love Him with our entire being and to love one another, and so for us, love is life—it is our reason, our passion and our vision forever.*

For many people, God's vision for a life of love can sound too good to be true, and so we need to ask: How can we know for sure that it is actually possible to love God with all our heart in this life?[10]

Deuteronomy 30:6, 11 (NASB)
"Moreover the LORD your God will circumcise your heart and the heart of your descendants, to love the LORD your God with all your heart and with all your soul, in order that you may live... For this commandment which I command you today is not too difficult for you, nor is it out of reach."

Apart from Christ, no one could love God with all their heart and soul. We are all just too broken, too selfish, too lost. But this is not our problem to solve—it is a problem for God and He has the answer. Here God backs up the greatest command with the greatest promise: **if we would devote our lives to loving Him with all our heart, God Himself will make it possible**. Because God cannot lie, this call is "not too difficult" for us, nor is it out of reach.[11] His word is His bond and it is our divine guarantee.

But is God really able to do it? Of course! God is all-powerful and so it is easy for Him to circumcise our hearts. But is He willing? He is not only willing, He is *longing* to fulfil this promise! So if the Father has both the power and the desire to make us wholehearted in our love for Him, what is stopping Him?

As with all the gifts of God, the gift of wholehearted love can only be received through faith. This means that God must wait until we come to the point of truly believing in His promise.[12] When we surrender our lives to the greatest command, we give God the permission He needs to perform His spiritual surgery on our hearts. Then, if we need cleansing, He will cleanse us. If our hearts need healing, He will heal us. If we need freedom, He will set us free. And if we need love, God will flood our lives with His love and restore our design so we can experience a flourishing life. The Father is ready, willing and able. When we finally say "yes" to the greatest command, God Himself will do whatever it takes to make His vision our reality.

Are you ready?

One Another

2

Ezekiel 36:27
"And I will put My Spirit within you and cause you to walk in My statutes and to carefully observe My ordinances."

Our journey into wholehearted love begins and ends with God. In this verse, the Father promises to fill us with His Spirit *so that* we can keep His commands. Not only does Jesus take away our sin and empty us of our selfishness through the cross, but He also fills us with His Spirit, which allows Jesus to keep the greatest command through us.

This gift of the Spirit means that we never need to generate our own love or strive in our own strength to keep the greatest command. We simply need to let Jesus make us "one spirit with Him."[13] When we enter into this unity, we step into the river of love that flows between the Son and the Father. In this place, instead of trying to keep the greatest command *for* Jesus, we start to keep it *with* Him. We let Jesus love the Father with all His heart through us and incredibly, His obedience is credited to us.

2 Peter 1:3-4 (BSB)
His divine power has given us everything we need for life and godliness through the knowledge of Him who called us by His own glory and excellence. Through these He has given us His precious and magnificent promises, so that through them you may become partakers of the divine nature, now that you have escaped the corruption in the world caused by evil desires.

In the Foreword, we looked at just a few of the great and magnificent promises in Scripture. We saw how God wants us to have the fullness of joy and to know a peace that surpasses all understanding. He wants to set us truly free so we can overcome our enemy.[14] He longs to lead us into a life of abundance, overflowing with the goodness and glory of God.[15] The fulfilment of these promises is not found so much in the gifts that God gives us but in the life of Christ within us. For Jesus has the fullness of joy.[16] He is the Prince of peace.[17] He is freedom and He always overcomes His enemy.[18] Jesus is our abundant, eternal life.[19] He is our goodness and our glory.[20] Jesus excels the sum of all beauty, and He comes to make our hearts His Eden—a place of surpassing beauty where He can not only visit, but where He can live forever.

The Father gives us these promises so that by them we can partake of the nature of Christ and grow in our union with Him. This union is the reason why John writes that the commands of God are not a burden.[21] Christ's yoke is easy and His burden is light because He carries the full weight of our obedience. His mission is to keep the greatest command and fulfil His vision for our lives, and our part is to let Him do it.

Our Corporate Design

Not long after Jesus defined God's design for us as individuals, He shared His vision for us as a corporate body of believers. He revealed it to His disciples in three simple words: *Love one another.*

> John 13:34-35
> "A new commandment I give to you, that you love one another: just as I have loved you, you also are to love one another. By this all people will know that you are my disciples, if you have love for one another."

Love one another. This one command gave the disciples everything they needed to know about church, including its nature, structure, mission and expression. Jesus has made love the essential motivation for our corporate life and it is as true for us now as it was for the Early Church back then. Why do we meet together? Love! Why do we praise God and worship together? Love! Why do we pray for one another, minister to one another, and give to meet each other's needs? *Love!!!* Now and forever, our corporate life is one of selfless love.

But does the new command now replace the greatest command? Is Jesus calling us to make people the focus of our love more than God?

Matthew 25:31-40

"When the Son of Man comes in his glory, and all the angels with him, then he will sit on his glorious throne. Before him will be gathered all the nations, and he will separate people one from another as a shepherd separates the sheep from the goats. And he will place the sheep on his right, but the goats on the left. Then the King will say to those on his right, 'Come, you who are blessed by my Father, inherit the kingdom prepared for you from the foundation of the world. For I was hungry and you gave me food, I was thirsty and you gave me drink, I was a stranger and you welcomed me, I was naked and you clothed me, I was sick and you visited me, I was in prison and you came to me.' Then the righteous will answer him, saying, 'Lord, when did we see you hungry and feed you, or thirsty and give you drink? And when did we see you a stranger and welcome you, or naked and clothe you? And when did we see you sick or in prison and visit you?' And the King will answer them, 'Truly, I say to you, as you did it to one of the least of these my brothers, you did it to me.'"

Here Jesus reveals that He and the Father do not sit in heaven and passively observe us as we go about our lives. Instead, because His Spirit lives within His people, Jesus is intimately and inescapably connected to us. Through His Spirit, Jesus experiences everything that we go through in life—He feels our hunger and our thirst, and He suffers every painful moment of our life with us. Just imagine it: Jesus humbles Himself to know us not merely in a theoretical way, but experientially by being aware of every emotion and every thought, and by being present with us in every single moment.

Just as Jesus participates in our pain, He also participates in the love that flows between us. As we eat together and encourage each other, as we value, honor and inspire one another, as we bring healing and joy to each other, our love is felt by the Spirit of Jesus more deeply than we could imagine. Knowing this, when He gave us the new command, Jesus was not replacing the greatest commands of loving God and loving our neighbor. Instead, He was beautifully weaving the two into one new command, revealing that **the primary way God wants to be loved is through His people.**

It is true that there is great blessing to be found in our times alone in our secret place, loving God and communing with Him in prayer, studying His word, waiting, watching, or giving Him praise. Our times of loving God on our own are a beautiful and necessary part of our relationship with Him, but they do not replace the call to love Jesus through His people.[22] We need to be rich in both personal and corporate love, and it helps to know why.

When we commune with God by ourselves, we are transformed and enriched by the love that flows, but it is often too easy to let that love end with our own blessing. In contrast, when we love Jesus through another person, not only are we blessed, but our love also changes the other person. It may bring healing, freedom, vision, inspiration, correction or hope— almost anything a person needs can be found in the love of God that flows through us. But it doesn't end there. Scripture calls us to pass on the blessings that we have received, so when we love someone, that person receives a love that they can then share with others.[23] As they let their newfound love flow to someone else, the other person is also filled with a measure of God's love that they can likewise share and multiply.

In this way, the call to love one another is an invitation to create a cascade of glory in the lives of the people around us. And just as powerful rivers can begin with only a trickle of water, even the smallest acts of love can have incredible unforeseen results. A kind word, a warm hug, a simple prayer, a heart-felt message, a thoughtful gift—an act of love that starts out small is quickly multiplied and amplified as it flows through many lives. Part of the beauty of this is that no matter how mature in Christ we are, any one of us can start a cascade of love at any time. Then, as we learn to love Jesus through His people, instead of ending with our own blessing, our love will ripple out through countless relationships to transform families, communities, and over time, perhaps even entire nations.

Believe and Love

1 John 3:23
This is His commandment, that we believe in the name of His Son Jesus Christ, and love one another, just as He commanded us.

Is it possible to follow Jesus and ignore the new command? We could as easily ask: is it possible to be a chef and not cook food or to be a firefighter and not fight fires? By definition, Christians are people who have put their faith in Jesus *and* who love one another.

Jesus did not die so that we could live a selfish Christian life, pursuing our own blessing while still looking forward to heaven after we die.[24] Christ's new command is that we love Him by loving one another. This is what it means to follow Jesus and so as His followers, we must wrestle with it. Like a chef confronted by the call to cook food, we must process the new command through to a conclusion. We must come to the point of either fully believing it and then devoting our lives to loving Jesus through one another or rejecting it and continuing to live for ourselves.

What will you do with the new command?

Children of God

3

Ephesians 1:3
Blessed be the God and Father of our Lord Jesus Christ, who has blessed us in Christ with every spiritual blessing in the heavenly realms.

In this verse we see the extravagant love of God. The Father, who did not withhold His only Son, still holds nothing back but gives us *every* spiritual blessing in Christ Jesus. By filling us with the Spirit of Jesus, God blesses us to share in all the different qualities of Christ's nature: His love, joy, peace and patience, His humility, gentleness, confidence and zeal, His goodness, compassion, mercy, freedom and so much more.

But do we experience all these blessings from the moment we first believe? Not remotely. Even now, many of us struggle to find any joy let alone the fullness of joy. Few seem to have taken hold of His surpassing peace, fewer still His powerful humility. It is all ours already, and yet we seem so strangely disconnected from the blessings that God has given to us in Christ Jesus. Where are we going wrong?

It is all a matter of relationship. God chooses to release His blessings through relationship which means that if we want to receive a specific blessing, we need to get to know God in a particular way. For example, if we want the blessing of wisdom, we need to get to know Jesus as our Teacher. If we want the blessing of provision, we need to get to know God as our Provider.

Just as our blessings in Christ are many and varied, so our relationship with God also has many depths to explore. God is our Creator, our Father, our Redeemer, and our King. He is our Stronghold, Deliverer, Leader, Protector, Comforter, Healer, Counsellor, and so much more. As we take the time to get to know God in these different ways, our unity with Him grows and we access more of His blessings in our life.

While all these relationships are always available to us, we do not experience them all from the moment we first believe. Instead, we find ourselves at the beginning of a journey with Jesus. Our first step is to know Christ as our Savior and receive the blessing of salvation. From there, the Holy Spirit leads us to relate to God in different ways. Having discovered Jesus as our Savior, we may go on to know Him as our Lord or Teacher or Friend or Healer or something else. The pace of our journey is usually determined by the level of our desire and engagement. At any time, we can settle for what we have received so far, or we can press on to know Him more. If we choose to keep seeking to know God in different ways, we'll find that each new relationship unlocks new realms of blessing and maturity in our lives.

It is the journey that changes us and so we need to resist the temptation to try and speed it up or leap ahead. No one matures in a moment and so it is fruitless to try to live as though we were 100 steps ahead of where we really are. Instead, we need to start where we are and let ourselves grow as we explore and learn, make mistakes and trip over and then get up again and keep on going. If we could skip the process of change and instead teleport to our destination, we would find ourselves as unarmed children on a battlefield intended for seasoned warriors. It is therefore essential that we come to value the journey and how it changes us by allowing us to get to know God in different ways. Every step has a purpose, and each one gives us more of the wisdom and maturity that we need for the road ahead.

In many Christian circles, people are taught to take the word of God and declare it into reality. It is important to give voice to the truth, but we cannot use it as a way of shortcutting the journey. Why? Because it doesn't work for relationships. We do not make Jesus our King by our words alone, but we enthrone Him as we learn to live in obedience to His voice. Likewise, it is meaningless to call God our Refuge if we keep on running to the world for our comfort. All the different relationships we can have with God are like this. Each one requires something of us if we are to know God in that particular way.

Our Father

1 John 3:1a (BSB)
Behold what manner of love the Father has given to us, that we should be called children of God. And that is what we are!

God created us and gave us life and so knowing Him as our Father is one of the most precious and foundational relationships we can have with Him. But do all believers relate to God as their Father? Sadly, no—but why not? It is because experiencing God as our Father requires something of us, something that not everyone is willing to give or to give up.

Jesus shows us what is needed in the parable of the prodigal son. In this story, both the elder and the younger son seek to earn the approval of their father, preferring to relate to him as a master rather than a father. The younger son did this through his desire to return as a servant, and the elder son from his mindset and lifestyle as a servant.

Through this parable, Jesus is showing us that to know God as our Father, we need to stop trying to earn His acceptance. Instead, we need to become convinced that God's love is a free gift that He will never sell to anyone, not for all the works in the world. Seeing God's love through this lens breaks us free from the bondage of legalism with its cycles of striving and failing and trying harder next time. It allows us to receive the Father's embrace and to rest in His unconditional love. As His beloved sons and treasured daughters, we can be secure in knowing that we never need to perform for our Father's attention—we have it already and always will.

For many people, this can be hard to accept at first. Like the prodigal son, many of us are so consumed by our own sense of failure that we feel compelled to work our way out of our unworthiness. Deep down we think that the only way we can be of value to God is if we can make ourselves useful to Him, so we pray, "*God use me! Let me be as one of your servants!*" We keep on trying to use our behavior as a currency to buy God's love, but it never works. Still we persist, and like the elder son in the parable, we end up living in spiritual poverty, surrounded by our own untouched wealth.

This is not what the Father wants for His children. His vision is for a life rich in love and joy, overflowing with every blessing in Christ Jesus! Yet this life only begins when we stop striving and allow ourselves to fall into the arms of our Father. Only there can we know that we are truly loved—unconditionally, eternally, infinitely loved.

Like Children

Matthew 18:1-3

At that time the disciples came to Jesus, saying, "Who is the greatest in the kingdom of heaven?" And calling to him a child, he put him in the midst of them and said, "Truly, I say to you, unless you turn and become like children, you will never enter the kingdom of heaven. Whoever humbles himself like this child is the greatest in the kingdom of heaven."

Here Jesus calls us to become like little children. Why? Because there is a purpose to our infancy. In the natural realm, the lifelong psychology of a person begins to form on day one. When a mother nurses her new baby, a physical and emotional bond forms between them. This connection allows the baby to develop a sense of security in the place of total dependency. For the baby, there is no need to strive and no pressure to earn affection. The baby just cries out for love and then receives it with pleasure.

This kind of bonding also takes place in our relationship with God. When we first come to faith in God, we are spiritually born again and like all babies, we crave the pure spiritual milk of God. As God feeds and nurtures us, we attach to Him and lay a foundation of love and unity for the life ahead.

No baby pays for their milk, and so it is in this phase of growth that we learn about grace. We discover that God gives us everything as a free gift. If we try to earn the gift, we prevent God from giving it to us for none of His blessings are for sale. So instead of working for God's approval, in our infancy, we learn how to receive His blessings by faith and relax into the way of grace.

When my children were young, they never worried about provision or thought, "I wonder if my parents will feed me today." In a healthy family, children are entirely secure in a place of complete dependency. The same is true spiritually. In our infancy, we need to get to know Jesus as our Shepherd and learn that as long as He leads us, we shall lack nothing. Our Father feeds the sparrows and clothes the lilies and He promises to take good care of us.[25]

When we learn to trust God and receive His provision in our infancy, a foundation is laid in our hearts that frees us to love others extravagantly. We can give without thought of self because we know that God will always provide everything we need. However, if we do not learn to depend on God when we are young, even though we may mature in other areas of life, we will continue to carry a level of doubt over God's provision that will constantly limit what God can do through us.

So if you grew up too quickly and have never learned to fully depend on God, then simply return to the place of childlike faith. Allow the Father to take you in His arms and to hold you. Learn to look to Him and receive His love and affection. Find an area in your life to truly depend on God and then watch as He meets your need. Repent from trying to earn His blessings by making yourself worthy of His promises. Let go of the fear of rejection and allow yourself to believe that you are born again as a child of God. There is now a place at the table just for you. You are a child of the Father and He loves you. He deeply, passionately, *eternally* loves you.

Church as a Family

4

1 Peter 1:22-23[26]

Since you have in obedience to the truth purified your souls for a sincere love of the brethren, fervently love one another from a pure heart, for you have been born again not of seed which is perishable but imperishable, that is, through the living and enduring word of God.

Since we have purified our souls *for* a sincere love of the brethren, we are to love one another fervently from a pure heart.

In this passage, the word *brethren* describes a family relationship and is used throughout the New Testament to address *all* believers.[27] Just as children are born into a family and siblings are forever connected by their DNA, so when we are spiritually born again, we are eternally connected not only to God as our Father, but to one another as a spiritual family. Above everything else, the church is a family.

But why is family so important to God? God Himself exists in a union of love as Father, Son and Spirit, and the family is the closest reflection we have of that unity on earth. God created the family to be a place where unconditional love flows and we can be real with each other without the threat of rejection. It is the place of the greatest transparency and deepest knowing. The family is a place of provision and protection and instruction, a place where we live in a culture of love and build our sense of identity together. Family is where we know that we will always be welcome home because we can never stop being a son or daughter. It is who we are and where we belong. And family is God's vision for His church.

The Call to Family

John 13:35

"By this all people will know that you are my disciples, if you have love for one another."

Jesus longs for us to be known in the world by our love for one another. But is the church worldwide seeking to fulfil His longing? Are we meeting, relating, and loving like a family?

Sadly no. But why not? In times past, many influential believers made it their goal to save as many people as possible. With the best intentions, they gathered masses of people but then placed the needs of the many upon the shoulders of the few. We inherited their vision and continued the tradition, perfecting the weekly service as an event that could cater for hundreds or thousands. But it came at a cost. Over the centuries, we evolved into an organization that was more like a spiritual orphanage than a loving family. We gathered great numbers of people, but love got lost in the crowd.

When the church lost her vision for family, we lost our identity. Instead of living as sons and daughters of God who are seen, heard, known and loved, most of us became like orphans in an audience: unseen, unheard, unknown and unloved. And this is not the leaders' fault. Most church leaders love God and are devoted to serving His people, but they only have so much time to give. They stand in the place of spiritual parents, but like managers in an orphanage, there are simply too many people needing their love. So they do their best. Many leaders sacrifice their own need for family and instead risk burnout as they pour their lives out for the people. Some leaders see the impossible nature of the task and resign themselves to just delivering the sermon and keeping people inspired enough to come back next week. Few take the time they need to truly apprehend the new command. Is this the kind of church that Jesus had in mind when He called us to love one another? Was this really His vision?

An Unchanging Vision

Christ's plan for His people has always been one of spiritual families who genuinely love each other and He will not change His mind. But why is God so intent on having us relate as a family?

Remember how we learned that the primary way Jesus wants to be loved is through His people. Jesus feels the love that flows between us and even the slightest expressions of love bring Him lasting joy. Christ's desire for our love will never wane, which is why He won't give up on His vision for us to become a loving family.

If we would view our relationships in this light, we would realize that every person that God has placed in our lives is uniquely valuable because each one allows us to love Jesus and receive His love in a unique way. When we truly believe this, we see how important it is that we learn to guard the health and holiness of our relationships. For if we allow misunderstanding or offense to stop the flow of love between us and another believer, then by doing so, we deny the Spirit of Jesus in that person the very love that Christ died for. It is therefore critical that we get this right. We must understand that when Jesus gives us the new command, He is not giving us some helpful advice or a new suggestion. He is giving us a command, and this makes it a matter of obedience for all believers. And because it applies to everyone, no matter what we have been through in life or how far we think we have fallen, no one is disqualified. We are all equally bound by Christ's command to find or form a loving spiritual family.

So what does family love look like? In a world so corrupt and broken, it can be hard to imagine giving and receiving a pure, selfless love. But Jesus would not command it if He was not willing to make it possible. So if we are going to embrace His vision for church, we cannot water down the call. We need to find a credible, attainable answer to this question: What does it look like to fervently love one another from a pure heart?

Love Poured Out

Romans 5:5

And hope does not disappoint us, because God has poured out His love
into our hearts through the Holy Spirit, whom He has given us.

As we embrace the new command, it is important to know that God does
not want us to act as though we are loving and neither does He expect us to
try and generate our own love. Instead, He wants to pour out *His love* into
our hearts so that we might become authentically loving people.

This love that God pours into us is not merely a sentimental emotion or
kind intention—it is the awesome force of Christ's nature within us that
flows through our words and our actions. In our words, we share God's love
through genuine encouragement, honest conversation, and vulnerable
prayer. We choose to see each person through God's eyes and to remind
people of who God created them to be. We seek to share Jesus' unwavering
optimism and to express His joy-filled delight in His people.[28]

For me, learning to give meaningful encouragement was like learning a
new language with a whole new vocabulary. I literally had to practice phrases
I could say to my children so they didn't sound awkward. For many people
like me, learning to speak from the heart can be a stretching experience, but
that is exactly what the Greek word translated as *fervent* means: fully
stretched. And while it may be hard at first, the good news is that the more
we stretch ourselves in love, the easier it becomes.

In our actions, we love people by sharing what we have to meet their
needs, and by blessing them and ministering to them. We love people by
empowering them in their calling, following the Lord as He shows us how to
act in ways that fulfil His vision and architect success in a person's life. We
can then go beyond the basics by getting to know someone so well that we
discover what brings them real joy and delight—what makes them feel alive.
We can then love them by orchestrating that joy in their life.

The Power of the Few

As we develop spiritual family, we will soon realize that the intimacy we experience is always connected to the size of the group. The more people we add to a group, the more we guard our hearts, which in turn limits our love. Conversely, when we meet in small numbers, love can flow in its full strength. In small groups, there is time and attention for everyone, and we can get to know each other. We can reveal our needs without any sense of shame, and we can then meet the needs of others in the group. When we are part of a small family, we are free both to love and to be loved.

But if we choose to run with Jesus' vision for family, should we then stop meeting in large numbers? *Not at all.* But it helps to know the purpose of large-scale meetings. The Early Church met in the temple to share the good news of Jesus with the people.[29] These meetings acted as a funnel to channel people into spiritual families where they could be loved and discipled in the faith. The Early Church also had large gatherings when the apostles visited so all the local believers could receive corporate teaching. In the same way, our large-scale services provide a place for us to receive teaching and to share times of praise and ministry. Yet while these are valuable in the life of believers, they do not replace the need for each person to be truly known and loved. For this need to be met, every believer needs to find their place in a spiritual family.

In summary, the purpose of the large corporate meeting is to:
- Share teaching, praise, testimony, and ministry
- Provide a place of witness for the world to hear the gospel
- Funnel people into spiritual families

In contrast, the purpose of the spiritual family is to:
- Know and love one another (and so keep the new command)
- Spur each other onto love and good works

- Fellowship together, sharing food and celebrating communion
- Nurture younger believers to a place of spiritual maturity
- Train and equip people to move in their giftings
- Minister to one another and meet each other's needs
- Empower people to move forward in their calling
- Multiply by creating more spiritual families

Inspire Family

If you are a pastor or leader of a large-scale church, please pray seriously about leading your people to become an assembly of spiritual families rather than a congregation of individuals. Inspire people to find their seat at the table and not just a pew before a stage. Activate spiritual parents. And make it clear that this is not just an appeal for more homegroups. Such groups have a defined function such as a Bible study, a prayer group, an outreach group, a worship group and so on. These are good, and spiritual families may do many of these things, but the primary purpose for a family meeting together will always be to know and love one another.

Finally, knowing that God is calling people back into family, do not be threatened or surprised when the Spirit of God moves outside the four walls of the church building. Instead, expect it. Encourage it. Empower it. Inspire it. Model it! Form your own spiritual family in which you can leave your title at the door and simply be loved for being you. Watch in awe as God transforms His people and revives your own life with the joy of family love.

Richard Halverson once said that Christianity started in the Middle East as a Christ-centered fellowship (a family). It went to Greece and became a philosophy, went to Rome and became an institution, went to Europe and became a culture, then went to America and became a business. Over the centuries we lost our way. It's time to return to love.

It's time to become a family once again.

Church on a Mission

5

Matthew 28:16-20
Now the eleven disciples went to Galilee, to the mountain to which Jesus had directed them. And when they saw him they worshiped him, but some doubted. And Jesus came and said to them, "All authority in heaven and on earth has been given to me. Go therefore and make disciples of all nations, baptizing them in the name of the Father and of the Son and of the Holy Spirit, teaching them to observe all that I have commanded you. And behold, I am with you always, to the end of the age."

In this passage, Jesus calls His disciples to make more disciples. This is often referred to as "the Great Commission" and it extends to all believers. As the church, our mission is to make disciples and teach them to observe His commands. So where do we start? Which commands of Christ are the most important to keep?

1 Peter 4:8 (NKJV)
And above all things have fervent love for one another, for "love will cover a multitude of sins."

Here Peter writes that the new command is to be our highest priority in life. Above everything else, God is calling us to fervently love one another and so this must be one of the foundational goals for our discipleship. But how can we disciple people into this kind of love if we are not genuinely living it ourselves?

Discipleship is not just about teaching the truth as a theory but about modelling it as an actual reality. After all, if discipleship is a journey, how can we lead someone to a place we haven't been? Only after we have come to forgive others can we testify to the healing power of forgiveness. Only after hearing the Spirit of God speak to us can we help others to discern His voice. In almost every respect, we can only impart to others those things that are already real for us. So if we are to take up the Great Commission, we must first embrace the Great Command and begin to outwork it in our own spiritual family. This is the first step of our mission.

Teaching to Observe

The deepest learning is not found in the head, but in the heart and hands. This is why Jesus calls us to teach new believers to *observe* His commands. Our actions flow from what our heart believes rather than our mind and so as we make disciples, we need to focus less on head-knowledge and more on heart-knowledge. This involves teaching new believers how to meditate on the word of God and let the Spirit write His truth on their hearts. As their hearts are then changed, it will then become natural for them to act in love and so live out Christ's commands.

Another key to heart-learning is to ask more questions than give answers. In Biblical times, a rabbi would teach people through constant questioning and interaction. We can see this in the life of Christ. In the gospels, Jesus asks hundreds of questions while rarely giving direct answers to any He is asked. This is a brilliant but often overlooked aspect of His discipleship. Jesus' questions invite us to explore our hearts and discover our real motivations. They arouse curiosity, inspire our imagination, create hunger, and help us to see with new vision. Jesus uses questions to open our hearts to the Father's Love. His questions call us to come, learn, trust, believe, to love, act, rest, and receive, to unite, grow, risk all and overcome.

When we teach merely to impart knowledge, that knowledge can be received or rejected by the learner. But when we ask questions, we plant seeds of curiosity which can inspire the person to wrestle with God and discover the Holy Spirit as the One who leads us into truth. He does this by taking us on a journey from teaching to revelation. This journey can take time, sometimes days or weeks or even months, but it is worth the wait. When the revelation comes, that truth becomes real for the person and they take ownership of it. Instead of being *our* teaching written on their minds, it becomes *their* revelation, written on their hearts.

When done this way, discipleship is more like mentoring than teaching. It is taking time to walk along the journey with a new believer and build a relationship where both the student and the teacher are known and loved. Because discipleship is so intensely relational, the ideal place to make new disciples of Jesus is one-on-one or in small groups.

A Place for Discipleship

In the First Great Awakening, John Wesley saw the need for discipleship to happen within spiritual families. In his journal, Wesley reflected on the long-term fruit of a Pembrokeshire revival that lacked any discipleship.

> "I was more convinced than ever that the preaching like an apostle, without joining together those that are awakened and training them up in the ways of God, is only begetting children for the murderer. How much preaching has there been for these twenty years all over Pembrokeshire! But no regular societies [small group meetings], no discipline, no order or connection; and the consequence is, that nine in ten of the once-awakened are now faster asleep than ever."[30]

Wesley knew that if new believers were not connected into small groups, the seed of the gospel would likely be stolen by the enemy. This still holds true today. If our focus is on making converts but not disciples, if there are no next steps for people to take, no water for the seed, no group to join, no family where a person can grow in the love of God, then new believers will often drift back to the world. When this happens, our evangelism itself can become a form of inoculation against the gospel. *I tried Christianity once, but it wasn't for me. I don't need to hear it all again.*

1 John 3:23
This is His commandment, that we believe in the name of His Son Jesus Christ, and love one another, just as He commanded us.

As we saw earlier, we cannot separate the call to faith from the call to love. So if we are inviting people to follow Jesus, we need to make it clear that this means both believing in Jesus and joining with other believers to learn how to love and be loved. The call to faith is a call to family.

Within family, discipleship is like spiritual parenting. It is the process of raising new believers up to maturity. And just like natural parenting, the nature of our parenting changes depending on the maturity of the new believer. When the person is young, we nurture, protect and care for them. As they grow, we empower, inspire and coach them. Then, when they attain maturity, we become more like friends and siblings. We encourage one another and form equal bonds of agape-love.

This process of growing up in Christ takes time. Unfortunately, the world wants everything now, and this craving for instant gratification can often spill over into our spirituality. So very few of us want to go on the journey to maturity. It seems too slow. So like the younger son, we turn to God and demand the fullness of our inheritance now so that we can spend it as we like. But we forget that character is not forged in a day. And without character, the riches of heaven are often wasted on self instead of being multiplied in the lives of others.

Therefore, when making disciples, we need to resist the temptation to race people through the different stages of spiritual growth. No good military commander would allow new recruits to skip basic training and go straight to the front lines. Instead, they put their soldiers on missions that match their level of ability and serve a specific purpose in their growth. The Spirit of God does the same thing for us. He knows that experience is a great teacher and He doesn't fear failure. So just as Jesus sent out the 72 to put into practice what they had learned, so the Holy Spirit sends us on assignments that are perfectly designed for our stage of growth. These assignments are a key feature of discipleship. They stretch us and grow us and give us a taste for a life of spiritual adventure.

For many people, adventure is the missing ingredient in their spiritual life. It balances our need for safety and intimacy with the need to take risks and reap rewards. We find intimacy within the safety of our spiritual family, but the real adventure comes as we hear the call of God to go into the world. It happens when we are on assignment in faraway lands and uncertain places. Adventure happens closer to home in the workplace and on the streets, in prisons, hospitals and at schools, in the halls of power and the tents of the homeless—anywhere that God is leading us to bring His love and presence.

When we have a strong spiritual family, we can confidently go forward on assignment, knowing our family will always be there in support. Some of them may even join the assignment with us. Then, when we return from each adventure, we can be refreshed by our family as we look forward to the next assignment.

This pattern of mission divides nicely into three repeating phases:
1. Preparing for our next assignment,
2. Going on the adventure of that assignment,
3. Reconnecting with family and being refreshed by their love.

Having tasted the joy of the mission, it can be tempting to see our assignments as our main area of fruitfulness in life. After all, that is where all the action seems to happen—people are saved, healed, inspired and transformed! For many of us, this is what makes us feel valuable in the kingdom of God, so we work hard to build a fruitful ministry. Yet we can become so focused on making an impact on the world that we fail to see where real fruitfulness comes from.

In John 15, Jesus calls us to abide in Him *so that we might be abundantly fruitful.* He then shows us how to do this: by loving one another. Jesus knows that it is the flow of His love that infuses our actions with true eternal value. We can have the faith to move mountains and preach the word to ten thousands, but without love it is all a waste of time. This is true for all our assignments—love comes first. It will always be this way. The Greatest Command always comes before the Great Commission, and even our smallest assignments will only have value if they flow from a lifestyle of love.

The Father can give us assignments that last an hour, a day, a week, a month, a year or even an entire lifetime. But whatever the nature of the mission, if we are to accomplish it without burning out or falling into compromise, we need to have a family behind us that is separate from our assignment, one that has no need for titles, no demands for ministry; one that is all about knowing and loving and little else. When we are in this kind of family, we can be secure in the knowledge that no matter what happens on assignment, our family will always have our back and there will always be a seat at the table waiting for us.

We live in a Christian world that exalts the commission but neglects the family that is critical to the commission's true success. It is time we learned how to do both well and make our assignments eternally fruitful. Who is your family and what is your assignment?

Church as a Temple

6

What makes us Christian?

I was once invited to speak in a small church. I took a whiteboard with me and drew a person with a circle of four friends around them. I then asked the people, "Imagine this is you and these are your closest friends. What do you experience on a relational level when you're in a group of four or five?" They filled half the whiteboard with answers such as friendship, love, connection, conversation, joy and so on. I drew some more circles around the first and said, "In this outer circle we have 200 people. What do you experience on a relational level when you're in a group of 200?" Silence. One person answered with a question: "Community?" I then pointed to the list they had made. "So why are we so intent on trying to get more and more people to come to our meetings, when it means sacrificing all these relational blessings? Why don't we assemble in a way that we can enjoy all those things? Let's try it now."

I then asked the people to move into small groups to discuss some questions and build relationship. But before beginning, I invited everyone to take a moment to honor Jesus by looking someone else in the eye and saying, "You know, Jesus is my Lord and my Savior!"

One of the most senior members of the church, whom we will call William, immediately stood up and declared, "Well that is the stupidest thing I've ever heard! You're just being judgmental! And the older I get, the more I realize: You can't be judgmental!"

The people in the service were stunned, trying to make sense of what was happening. Why would this man be so opposed to confessing Jesus as his Lord?

The answer was simple. William was angry because he could not look someone else in the eye and say that Jesus was his Lord and Savior. Why not? Because it wasn't true. Willaim had been a part of the fellowship for decades and most people assumed he was a Christian because he faithfully attended church every Sunday. But his relationship was with the church and not with Jesus. It was only when he was challenged to affirm Christ's lordship that everyone saw the truth. William believed in Jesus, but he didn't know Him. Jesus was neither His Lord nor His Savior. He was his own lord, and now he was found out.

William died only two weeks later, but God's mercy prevailed. The Father told a friend to go to the hospital and minister to William only a day or two before he passed. They prayed and he was reconciled to God. After a lifetime of separation, the Father had His lost child back in His arms forever and love won again.

William's story raises an important question: what is it that makes us Christian?

A Temple of the Spirit

1 Corinthians 6:19
Or do you not know that your body is a temple of the Holy Spirit who is in you, whom you have from God, and that you are not your own?

2 Corinthians 13:5 (BSB)
Examine yourselves to see whether you are in the faith; test yourselves. Do you not realize that Jesus Christ is in you—unless you fail the test?

What defines us as being Christian is not our church attendance. It is not our view on morality or our political opinions. It is not even our intellectual belief in Jesus. The test of faith is a question of possession: does the Spirit of Jesus live within you? All other questions flow from this one reality. Is He in you? Do you know Him? Are you a temple for His Spirit?

Galatians 4:18-19
It is always good to be made much of for a good purpose, and not only when I am present with you, my little children, for whom I am again in the anguish of childbirth until Christ is formed in you! I wish I could be present with you now and change my tone, for I am perplexed about you.

Ephesians 3:14-17
For this reason I bow my knees before the Father, from whom every family in heaven and on earth is named, that according to the riches of his glory he may grant you to be strengthened with power through his Spirit in your inner being, so that Christ may dwell in your hearts through faith…

Both the Galatian and the Ephesian believers had received the Spirit of God. So why would Paul labor in prayer to see the life of Christ formed in the people? Didn't they already have Jesus in their hearts?

Our union with Christ is a gift that we receive by faith and is sustained by faith. The Galatian believers were falling into legalism by putting their trust in their own works rather than in the Spirit of Jesus within them. This rejection of faith caused them to let go of grace and close their hearts to the Holy Spirit. This had a devastating effect on their union with Jesus. By abandoning the way of grace, Paul writes that the Galatians were severing themselves from Jesus.[31] He calls the people to turn away from legalism and return to grace so that their union with Jesus could be restored and Christ might dwell in their hearts through faith once again.

The life we share with Jesus is a never-ending journey into an ever-deepening unity that differs significantly between infancy and maturity. We know that no one becomes instantly Christlike the moment they first believe and so we do not judge children by the standards of adults. Instead, we extend them grace. In the same way, we need to have grace for our own journey. We need to resist the temptation to condemn ourselves for lacking mature fruit or question our possession of Christ when we are still young in the faith. The main thing is that we are growing with Jesus and being possessed more and more by His Spirit. This is what makes us His temple.

A Place of Encounter

In Biblical times, people worshipped at temples because they believed that was where they encountered their god. If someone wanted to worship the goddess Diana then they would go to the temple of Diana because that was where the people believed she would manifest her presence and receive people's offerings. All the Greek and Roman gods had their temples or altars. But not the Christians. They were different. As the Early Church was beginning, the apostles were given more than enough money to build a great temple for Jesus, but they didn't want or need one. Why not? Because unlike all the other gods, their God chooses to live within His people.

This was and still is an incredibly radical, confronting belief. *The Spirit of God lives within His people.* If we only believed it, our lives would be gloriously transformed, for we would know that the same Spirit that lived in Jesus now lives in us and in other believers. *The same Spirit.* So even if only two or three of us meet together, no matter where we are—in a home, a park, an office, a café, or a church building—as a living temple of the Spirit we bring the presence of God into every space.

A Holy Place

In the Old Testament, the temple was a place of holiness, made up of an outer court, the Holy Place, and the inner sanctuary which was known as the Holy of Holies. The Hebrew word *qodesh* translated as *holy* means sacred, purified or set apart. The equivalent Greek word *hagios* means to be set apart for the use intended by its designer.[32] If we look at holiness through the metaphor of the clock, even though a clock may be flawless and perfectly free from any blemish, it only becomes truly holy when it fulfills its design by keeping the time. So there are three key qualities of holiness:

1. **Being consecrated**: setting ourselves apart from the world to live in union with Christ and to do the will of the Father
2. **Being purified**: allowing the blood of Jesus to fully cleanse our hearts of all sin, selfishness and unrighteousness[33]
3. **Living in Design**: allowing the Spirit to fill our hearts with His presence and to restore God's design for our lives

If we were to think of holiness only in terms of purity, we would see it as the absence of obvious sins such as pride, lust, greed, rage, gluttony and so on. But to discover the full nature of holiness, we need to ask: which sin is the greatest? Which sin impacts Jesus the most?

The metaphor of the clock can help us to answer this question. For what would be our clock's greatest sin? Because a clock is created to tell the time, its greatest sin must be *not telling the time*. So now what is our greatest sin?

John 13:34
"A new commandment I give to you, that you love one another: just as I have loved you, you also are to love one another."

As we learned earlier, the Father created us to love Jesus through one another. This is our design and so it is the defining standard of holiness. Because this is what God made us for, our greatest sin can only be *not loving one another*. This is the sin that impacts Jesus the most. With every selfish act and every isolating choice, we reject the Spirit of Jesus in His people and deny Him our love. This lovelessness compromises our holiness and defiles our temple. If we are to be a holy people, we must discover the power of the blood of Jesus to fully cleanse our hearts. It is time to learn that holiness is not just the grace that covers sin, but the love of Christ that flows from our hearts through our relationships to fill the world with His glory.

1 Thessalonians 3:11-13

Now may our God and Father himself, and our Lord Jesus, direct our way to you, and may the Lord make you increase and abound in love for one another and for all, as we do for you, so that he may establish your hearts blameless in holiness before our God and Father, at the coming of our Lord Jesus with all his saints.

Here Paul prays that the Lord would make us abound in love for one another *so that* He might establish our hearts blameless in holiness before the Father. Through the Scripture, we again hear the voice of the Spirit declaring that apart from love there can be no holiness, for holiness is love.

1 John 4:16

God is love, and whoever abides in love abides in God, and God abides in him.

John 15:10-12

"If you keep my commandments, you will abide in my love, just as I have kept my Father's commandments and abide in his love. These things I have spoken to you, that my joy may be in you, and that your joy may be full. This is my commandment, that you love one another as I have loved you."

1 John 4:7

Beloved, let us love one another, for love is from God, and whoever loves has been born of God and knows God.

As a temple, we are a place of habitation where we live in God and He lives in us. Because God is love, more than anything else, the Spirit of Jesus lives in us as a Spirit of Love. In this place of two-way abiding, Jesus shares His thoughts of love with us and infuses us with His will to love. He inspires us to speak words of love, and to act in love by doing good to others. It is the presence of this ever-increasing divine love within us that is the ultimate test of faith and the standard of what it means to be a mature Christian. In union with the Holy Spirit, we are love.

Becoming a Temple

1 Peter 2:5
You yourselves like living stones are being built up as a spiritual house, to be a holy priesthood, to offer spiritual sacrifices acceptable to God through Jesus Christ.

So how does a church become a holy temple?

One stone does not make a temple, just as one person does not make a family. Our journey into holiness therefore begins in community as we come together and set ourselves apart to God. As we lay our selfishness on the altar, the fire of God falls, and the blood of Jesus purifies our hearts. He then fills us with more of His Spirit and teaches us how to abide in Him by loving one another.

It is worth noting that each stone in the physical temple would have only been connected to five or six other stones. Like those stones, we only have the capacity for deep, meaningful connection with a handful of other believers. But that is all we need—a few is enough. As we are faithful to bind ourselves to one another, not only will we know the joy of being known and loved within our spiritual family, but we will find ourselves built together into a far greater and more beautiful whole: an eternally living temple of the Spirit of Jesus.

Church as a Body

7

John 17:20-23

"I do not ask for these only, but also for those who will believe in me through their word, that they may all be one, just as you, Father, are in me, and I in you, that they also may be in us, so that the world may believe that you have sent me. The glory that you have given me I have given to them, that they may be one even as we are one, I in them and you in me, that they may become perfectly one, so that the world may know that you sent me and loved them even as you loved me."

Only hours before the cross, Jesus prays His deepest desire: that we would be one with Him and one with each other. But in a Christian world with countless denominations and such varying doctrines, it's hard to see how this prayer could ever be answered. And yet Jesus could never pray a futile prayer. He always prays the Father's will and the Father always hears Him. Therefore, we can be sure that sooner or later, the Father is going to answer this prayer by raising up a people who are willing to become one. Then the world will know that the Father sent Jesus and that He loves us just like He loves Jesus—with an awesome, limitless, everlasting love.

But will we be among those believers who become one? Or will we defy Christ's prayer, forfeit the glory, and instead let ourselves be divided by our differing styles and theologies? The stakes are high and so take a moment to reflect. Imagine the honor of being a part of the Father's answer to Christ's prayer in this passage! Imagine the joy! Imagine the adventure of going on this journey into unity! The Father is offering us an incredible gift and if we are willing, He will do whatever it takes to bring us into union with Him and with each other. He made the Early Church of one heart and soul, and He wants to do it again.

One Body

1 Corinthians 12:12-27

For just as the body is one and has many members, and all the members of the body, though many, are one body, so it is with Christ. For in one Spirit we were all baptized into one body—Jews or Greeks, slaves or free—and all were made to drink of one Spirit.

For the body does not consist of one member but of many. If the foot should say, "Because I am not a hand, I do not belong to the body," that would not make it any less a part of the body. And if the ear should say, "Because I am not an eye, I do not belong to the body," that would not make it any less a part of the body. If the whole body were an eye, where would be the sense of hearing? If the whole body were an ear, where would be the sense of smell? But as it is, God arranged the members in the body, each one of them, as he chose. If all were a single member, where would the body be? As it is, there are many parts, yet one body.

The eye cannot say to the hand, "I have no need of you," nor again the head to the feet, "I have no need of you." On the contrary, the parts of the body that seem to be weaker are indispensable, and on those parts of the body that we think less honorable we bestow the greater honor, and our unpresentable parts are treated with greater modesty, which our more presentable parts do not require. But God has so composed the body, giving greater honor to the part that lacked it, that there may be no division in the body, but that the members may have the same care for one another. If one member suffers, all suffer together; if one member is honored, all rejoice together.

Now you are the body of Christ and individually members of it.

In this passage, Paul uses the metaphor of a body to show us what unity looks like in the church. In our physical bodies, there is awe-inspiring complexity involving countless interdependencies. From the heart to the brain, lungs, skin and bones, eyes and ears and mouth and nose—every single part of our body has a unique role that is needed for us to be healthy.

The interconnected nature of the body beautifully expresses Christ's unchanging vision for His church, one in which every person has a valuable part to play in the corporate life of the church. But who really believes it? Can we honestly say that everyone has an essential role in our fellowship? If not, then how do we respond to this passage?

When they read Paul's letter, early believers would have had the same questions and would have also found this new design for church intensely confronting. Having come to faith in Jesus, they would likely have assumed to meet in the style of Judaism where priests did the ministry on behalf of the people who spent most of the time observing the service. But instead God was calling *everyone* to be involved, even women![34] No one could sit back and passively watch while others did all the ministry. Knowing that this would require a whole new way of meeting and relating, Paul often used the body metaphor throughout his letters. He constantly challenged people to forge unity by involving everyone in the life of the church.

Excel in Building Up

Romans 12:4-8

Just as each of us has one body with many members, and not all members have the same function, so in Christ we who are many are one body, and each member belongs to one another. We have different gifts according to the grace given us. If one's gift is prophecy, let him use it in proportion to his faith; if it is serving, let him serve; if it is teaching, let him teach; if it is encouraging, let him encourage; if it is giving, let him give generously; if it is leading, let him lead with diligence; if it is showing mercy, let him do it cheerfully.

1 Corinthians 12:4-7

Now there are varieties of gifts, but the same Spirit; and there are varieties of service [ministries], but the same Lord; and there are varieties of activities, but it is the same God who empowers them all in everyone. To each is given the manifestation of the Spirit for the common good.

God gives His people a variety of gifts, ministries and activities, but it is the same Spirit who empowers them all *in everyone*. The ministry blessings are not just for those in leadership but for every single believer, *including you*. God has given you a manifestation of the Spirit that your spiritual family genuinely needs and until you start to function in it, the people in your fellowship won't be able to experience the abundant life that God so desires for them. It is therefore essential that you take your place in the body of Christ and start to minister to others. Your people need you.

Looking Back at the End

So what happens if you don't find your place in the body? I once talked to a woman in her final year of life. She was a talented, loving and generous person. Despite having raised a beautiful family, she said, "I don't want a big funeral with people standing up and lying about all the good things I've done because the truth is that I haven't done anything for the Lord."

I felt like she was looking back on her journey through life and seeing just how little she had used her unique gifts to encourage others in the body. Like the servant who buried his master's gold, her spiritual talents had been buried in the pews. And it wasn't for a lack of desire. Like so many people, she wanted to be used by God to bless others, but there was simply no opportunity. Her church didn't recognize the value of small groups and the weekly service could not provide space for people to minister to each other.

So week after week, she sat faithfully through service after service, quietly burying her gifts next to people who could not see her value or feel the waste.

Her story is one that will be constantly repeated in people's lives unless we make a change. If we are in any form of leadership then we need to know that God has entrusted us with stewarding the gifts of the people in our fellowship. And one day we will be accountable to Him. So let's act now and help everyone to find their role within the body.

Each One

1 Corinthians 14:26
What then, brothers? When you come together, each one has a hymn, a lesson, a revelation, a tongue, or an interpretation. Let all things be done for building up.

Here Scripture directs us to meet in a way that allows people to minister to one another. Rather than a large-scale service, this kind of meeting calls for a smaller, more intimate gathering. Knowing this, the Early Church held meetings primarily in their homes. By limiting numbers, they created space for each person to bring something from God to encourage other believers. Like a family around the dining table, everyone had a voice, and everyone had something valuable to share that the others needed to receive.

It can be the same in our time. We can help each other to discover the unique giftings that God has given each of us. We can then come together in small groups and practice using our gifts. We don't have to be scared or feel the pressure to perform. No one begins in a place of perfection, and so a key reason why we practice is to learn from our mistakes. This requires humility and grace and an outright refusal to give in to the fear of failure. But if we all do this together, it won't be long before we start to become a healthy, vibrant body of believers.

So what are your giftings, ministries or activities? What is your role in the body? From teaching to hospitality, from prophecy to encouragement, from the discernment of spirits to giving, there are many spiritual as well as practical gifts, and all are valuable. Likewise, there are many ministries and few require a stage. In fact, most ministries operate best in a one-on-one or small group context where people feel loved and their hearts are open to receive. In these settings, the gifts can beautifully flow through our words as our conversations turn into prayers.

Need to Need Each Other

In our physical body, every part depends on the other parts working for its own life and function. In the same way that a hand needs a wrist and the wrist needs an arm and no part can say to another, "I have no need of you," so it is for us. Like a body, God has designed us for dependency. He has intentionally tied our spiritual prosperity to the welfare of the other people in our fellowship so that we all flourish together or struggle alone.

Jesus establishes this mutual need for each other at the most basic level through the command to love one another. No one can obey this command on their own for how can we love others without others? The truth is we can't. Trying to pursue a righteous life in isolation is like a being a dismembered hand that is more concerned with having perfect skin and nails than it is with the blood that brings it life! It is far better to be an imperfect hand connected to an imperfect body than a flawless hand that is severed and dying. Knowing this, if we want to be the answer to Christ's prayer for unity, we must be willing to surrender our independence and humbly accept our need for one another.

At first it may be hard to see how we need others. In their infancy, some people may not contribute much to the wider body. But if we help them practice using their gifts and give them time to mature, we can be sure that they will soon develop a personal ministry that others genuinely need.

When we see the potential in others, we will realize that the greatest good we can do for the body of Christ is to not just to function in our own gifts but to empower others to function in theirs. As each person steps into their own unique ministry, the life will soon spread to every part of the body and we will find the unity that Jesus is so fervently praying for.

Gifts with Love

1 Corinthians 13:2

And if I have prophetic powers, and understand all mysteries and all knowledge, and if I have all faith, so as to remove mountains, but have not love, I am nothing.

In Christ, we are all baptized into one body in which His love flows like blood to bring life and healing to every part of the body. If love is not flowing, we are not living; we are nothing more than a pile of dry bones. It is therefore important to remember that our value is not found simply in the operation of the gifts, but in the love that flows through them. For as Scripture says: even if we have prophetic powers, understand all mysteries, and have all knowledge, *without love we are nothing*. Therefore, if we have the gift of teaching, we should not think of ourselves as a teacher who sometimes loves but as a lover of Christ who sometimes teaches. Love is to be the defining force of who we are and everything we do. For without love we are nothing, but with love, we are something inexpressibly valuable both to God and to others.[35]

If the idea of having a role in the body sounds overwhelming, take heart: it's not too difficult for you. In fact, Christ's vision for church is easier than anyone would imagine. Why? Because God has made everything to flourish when it lives in His design. If we take a plant and give it light and water and nutrients, it will naturally flourish and reveal its full beauty to the world. The same is true for church. If we meet together like a body as God always intended, our gatherings will never be dull or boring, but they will be inspiring, joyful, unpredictable, and effortlessly beautiful.

Church as a Bride

8

Ephesians 5:31-32

"Therefore a man shall leave his father and mother and hold fast to his wife, and the two shall become one flesh." This mystery is profound, and I am saying that it refers to Christ and the church.

In Scripture, God presents His design for church in many ways. He wants us to become a spiritual family, a place of mission, a temple of His Spirit, and a living body. Yet beyond all these things is the Father's ultimate vision: that we would all become a bride worthy of His Son.

In Chapter Three, we saw how our spiritual life is a journey of relationship with God. Over the course of the journey, we come to know God as our Father, our King, our Refuge, our Protector, our Provider, our Champion and so much more. We likewise discover Jesus as our Redeemer, our Lord, Teacher, Shepherd, Friend, and more. Each relationship reveals a different aspect of God's heart and contains its own unique blessings.

As we learned earlier, we do not encounter God in all these ways when we first choose to follow Jesus. Instead, each depth of relationship is given to us as a gift that we can choose to receive or reject. We only receive and unwrap each gift as we learn how to relate to God in that particular way.

This takes time and can be stretching, but it is a key to our spiritual growth. For each dimension of relationship helps us to mature by requiring something of us. To know Jesus as our Savior requires us to have faith in Him and to accept the gift of salvation without trying to earn it. To know

Christ as our King requires a willingness to obey His voice. To know Jesus as our Teacher, we need to become like a student and learn how to study and apply His teachings. To know Christ as our Friend requires us to learn how to honestly share our hearts with Him. Every relationship we can have with God calls for our participation in a unique way.

The Bridegroom

John 3:29

"The one who has the bride is the bridegroom. The friend of the bridegroom, who stands and hears him, rejoices greatly at the bridegroom's voice. Therefore this joy of mine is now complete."

John the Baptist describes Jesus as the Bridegroom who has the bride. God has given every believer the gift of knowing Jesus as their Bridegroom, but do we all encounter Him in this way? No, but why not? It is because this dimension of relationship requires something of us that many people are not yet ready to give.

The key to experiencing this level of relationship with Jesus is revealed in the metaphor of *the bride*. By definition, a bride is someone who has made a covenant to love one man at the exclusion of all others. She has surrendered her singleness and devoted her life to living in unity with her husband. This is what it means to be a bride, and it is precisely why Scripture uses it to describe our relationship with Jesus. The Bible does not use the term *bride* lightly, and it is not just another name for *church*. Jesus uses the metaphor of marriage because it speaks of a relationship of love, devotion, intimacy, transparency and unity, all built on the foundation of a lifelong, life-defining covenant.[36] This is the Father's glorious vision for every believer *and especially you*. If we want to know Jesus in this way, we need to step into our identity as His bride and let the Spirit prepare our hearts for covenant love.

Journey into Covenant Love

Ezekiel 16:8 (NKJV)

"When I passed by you again and looked upon you, indeed your time was the time of love; so I spread My wing over you and covered your nakedness. Yes, I swore an oath to you and entered into a covenant with you, and you became Mine," says the Lord GOD.

In Ezekiel 16, Scripture tells the story of Isarel's growth from infancy to maturity, which parallels our own spiritual growth in Christ. Apart from Christ, we are all alone, slowly dying in our sin. Yet the Father sees us, stops, and speaks life over us. By His grace, we are born again as children of God, but as infants in Christ, our knowledge of God and our capacity for love is limited. Over time, we get to know God and experience His love in different ways. We discover God as our Father, Provider, Defender and more, and the blessings that flow from these relationships all change our heart. We continue to grow and mature until we reach our time of love—the day when we are finally ready to make a covenant with Jesus.

This covenant of love is not like a contract that may be in effect just for a season. When we become His bride, we devote ourselves to living in unity with Jesus *for the rest of our lives*. This is something that changes us at the deepest level—it reshapes our sense of identity and defines our life going forward. When we make this covenant, our life of singleness ends, and a new realm of union begins. It is no longer *I* but *We* forever.

Hosea 2:16, 19-20 (BSB)

"In that day," declares the LORD, "you will call Me 'my Husband,' and no longer call Me 'my Master.' For I will remove from her lips the names of the Baals; no longer will their names be invoked.

"...So I will betroth you to Me forever; I will betroth you in righteousness and justice, in loving devotion and compassion. And I will betroth you in faithfulness, and you will know the LORD."

Romans 7:4 (NKJV)

Therefore, my brethren, you also have become dead to the law through the body of Christ, that you may be married to another—to Him who was raised from the dead, that we should bear fruit to God.

Earlier we learned that if we are to know God as our Father, we have to stop relating to Him as our Master. In the same way, if we are to know Jesus as our Bridegroom, we must die to the law. Every trace of legalism in our hearts and every mindset that would seek to make ourselves worthy of His affection or to earn His love—it all must utterly die. Only then can we be free to know Jesus as our Bridegroom.

It is important to note that the call to become the bride of Christ has nothing to do with our sexuality. Men don't have to deny their masculinity or become feminine in any way to be the bride. Scripture uses the metaphor of marriage solely because it is a relationship of covenant and union. It has nothing to do with gender or sexual attraction. Therefore all of us are called to this relationship because we are all equally called to make a covenant of love with Jesus.[37]

So what does that covenant look like?

Highest Devotion

Matthew 22:34-40

But when the Pharisees heard that he had silenced the Sadducees, they gathered together. And one of them, a lawyer, asked him a question to test him. "Teacher, which is the great commandment in the Law?" And he said to him, "You shall love the Lord your God with all your heart and with all your soul and with all your mind. This is the great and first commandment. And a second is like it: You shall love your neighbor as yourself. On these two commandments depend all the Law and the Prophets."

Here Jesus sums up the entire Law and reveals that all Scripture is based on the commands to love God with our entire being and to love others. Many theologians believe that God gave the Law to the people of Israel as a ketubah or wedding covenant. Through this lens, the greatest command is like a wedding vow that commits us to a life of love and union with Jesus.

The great command also shows us what Jesus is looking for in His bride. He does not want to share us with the world or to have a casual relationship with us. He wants all of us: all our heart, all our soul, all our mind, and our entire life. He wants to be our passion, our vision, and our reason for being. This is God's highest will for our lives and if we let Him, the Father will share His love for Jesus with us and make us a bride of inexpressible beauty for His Son.[38]

While God has invited all believers to make this covenant with Jesus, we learn in Scripture that many people will reject the invitation. In Matthew 22, Jesus shares the parable of a king who sends out messengers to invite people to a great wedding feast for his son. But the people have given their hearts to lesser things. They refuse to come, and the king is both heartbroken and enraged.

Sadly the same thing is happening today. The Father longs to present us to Jesus as a bride worthy of His Son, but He can't force His will upon us—it has to be a truly free and loving choice on our part. So all the Father can do is wait for our agreement. How will we respond to the invitation? It will cost us everything to say *yes* and even more to say *no*. And yet none of us want to break the Father's heart or miss out on our inheritance. So let's focus on this one thing and make ourselves ready. Let's work through our resistances, abandon our idols, and refuse to make any excuse that would keep us from fully responding to Jesus. Let's join with the Spirit to forge a heart that is willing to say *Yes* and *I do* to Jesus.

Like a bride at the altar, when we say *yes* to Jesus, we step into a whole new life of love, intimacy and unity with Christ. If in your own journey, you have reached your time of love, make a covenant with Him by saying something like:

"Jesus, I devote my entire life and future to loving You and living in unity with You. I turn away from every idol and renounce all my affections for the world. I can't do this alone, but I know that You died to make me Your bride and that nothing is impossible for You. So if You will help me to do it, I will love You with all my heart, soul, mind and strength. I choose to be one with You forever!"

It's that simple. This prayer gives the Holy Spirit the permission He needs to prepare us as a bride worthy of God's Son. This is the highest desire of the Father for every believer and for the entire church worldwide. We were born for this. Our Love is waiting. Are you ready to come away with Him?

***

If you sense that this now is the time for you to discover Jesus as your bridegroom, please read "Bride Arise" available at onewithchrist.org.

Church as a Net

9

Matthew 16:18

"And I tell you, you are Peter, and on this rock I will build my church, and the gates of hell shall not prevail against it."

When Jesus said He would build His church, He had a specific design in mind. Jesus revealed His plan to the disciples who then carried it out by creating an expansive network of spiritual families that we call the Early Church. These spiritual families met together to fulfil a single common vision: to love one another.

To make His vision possible, Jesus poured out His Spirit into His people, giving them access to a limitless supply of love. The early believers became a river of God's love as they started sharing their hearts, their lives and their resources with one another. They formed deep and meaningful relationships, they ministered to one another, and they gave what they had to meet each other's needs. Put simply, they became a family.

The love that flowed between early believers created such a unity that Scripture says they became "of one heart and soul."[39] These believers did not see the call of love as a duty or obligation, but as a way of life that is fueled by supernatural joy. Within these spiritual families, early believers learned how to live in God's design of love and so they flourished. Even in places of spiritual desolation and through times of horrific persecution, the Early Church continued to grow. These believers poured their lives out in love and overwhelmed the world, changing it for millennia to come. The power of love was unstoppable!

48

Net of Fire and Gold

God's plan for His people has not changed, and *it will never change*. Just as it was back then, so even now God remains committed to seeing His church become a network of loving families.

A friend once shared a vision of these spiritual families with me.[40] He said, "God showed me a picture of fires burning all over New Zealand. I zoomed in on one of the fires and saw that it was a small group of people. A golden thread of love wove from heart to heart, connecting each person to the others in the group. Different threads then went out from those people to the hearts of other people in nearby groups. I zoomed out and I could see the whole country covered by a net of fire and gold."

Another friend shared a similar vision of how she also saw a net of gold over New Zealand. Something like a meteor crashed into it, but instead of breaking it, the energy of the impact rippled out across the whole net, which shook briefly but then settled down again. The net was unbreakable.

In a family, everyone gives to meet each other's needs, and because we are all extended family in Christ, this principle of giving works across the entire net. When a spiritual family or a group of families suffer need, the rest of the net can come together to provide for that need.

We see this kind of love in action in Scripture. When the Great Famine was prophesied, believers in Antioch and beyond started giving what they could to meet the needs of those in Jerusalem.[41] The Early Church network was alive with the love of God and just as it was back then, so it can be now.

Philippians 4:19
And my God will supply every need of yours according to his riches in glory in Christ Jesus.

Here God promises to supply all our needs. While sometimes He may keep this promise through miracles, most often He brings His supply through people. Why? Because generosity has a powerful way of creating unity between believers. As we look outward and start to practically love others in the wider body of Christ, we create a unity the forges strength in the net as a whole. At the same time, we open channels of relationship through which the Lord can supply our needs in the future.

It should be noted that while this culture of giving in the Early Church was a powerful witness to the world, it also created some problems by being attractive to lazy people who wanted to receive but not give. Paul addressed this writing, "If anyone is not willing to work, let him not eat." [42] Every able person was called to do honest work so that each one may have something to share with others in genuine need.[43] So like the Early Church, we are not to tolerate laziness or the abuse of generosity, but rather empower everyone to work and discover the joy of giving.

Growing the Net

The family unit is a relational structure that is designed to grow through multiplication rather than just addition. As our youngest daughter was getting ready to be married, a friend asked me, "Are you sad to see her go? After all these years, how do you feel about giving her away?"

"Are you kidding?! We spent her whole life preparing her to be a stunning wife and an amazing mother. And now she's ready. This was always our vision for her. We are thrilled to see her go and start her own family!"

One of the goals of a healthy family is to raise up the next generation, bringing infants to maturity and seeing them marry and multiply by having their own family. This is exactly what happened with the Early Church. New believers were discipled and as they matured in Christ, they were sent out to create new families of faith. We can see this in the life of Paul. He and Barnabas were elders in Antioch who were then sent out to share the gospel.[44] They formed new families of faith, discipled new believers, and appointed elders to oversee the spiritual families. These families multiplied and the cycle repeated. This is how the net spread and the Early Church changed the world.

In modern times, many fellowships multiply by dividing the group. Like a cell, they split apart and then let the new groups grow and divide again. However, this approach separates people from their closest friends. A potentially better approach is to send out a few mature believers to start a new family while also remaining a part of the original group. This allows those leaders to keep receiving love and encouragement from their original spiritual family while they pour their love into the new group.

John 13:35
"By this all people will know that you are my disciples, if you have love for one another."

Jesus longs for us to become known in the world by our love for one another because this is what lost souls yearn for. When an unbeliever only knows the love of the world, seeing the love of God is an awe-inspiring experience. I once brought a hitchhiker to a friend's place for dinner one night as we travelled down the country. We all talked and ate and enjoyed each other's company. It was a beautifully ordinary evening for us, but it left the young man overwhelmed by what he saw and felt. Later that evening, he said, "If this is Christianity, I have to find out more. I want this kind of love in my life."

God's ordinary is the world's extraordinary. The love that the Spirit of Jesus pours into our hearts is so different from anything the world knows. It sacrifices joyfully. It sees the real person and calls them into their true identity. It is extravagant, generous, patient, kind, relentlessly optimistic, and it does not tolerate division or offense. God's love always forgives and restores. It brings healing, wholeness, and a sense of reviving joy.

It is no wonder why love is the key to evangelism. When the world sees how we relate together and how we value one another, their hearts will bear witness to their own deep need for love. They will be drawn to Christ and born again into a family in which they will be raised as sons and daughters of the living God. With time, they will grow to maturity and then start their own family. In this way, the net will continue to spread across the world, overwhelming this present darkness with the most glorious light.

The Vision

In summary, we believe that the Lord is restoring His design for His people. Individually, He is teaching us how to put the first command into first place. He is healing our brokenness, taking away our selfishness, filling us with His Spirit, and leading us into a new way of life founded on love and unity with Him.

Corporately, God is restoring His design for church by giving us one new vision based on one new command: to love one another. He is teaching how to fulfill His vision by forging true spiritual family. At the same time, Jesus is making us a living temple—a place where the world can encounter God's presence and see the radiance of His love. The Father is also giving us all gifts and empowering us to function together as a connected body of believers. And above all this, through the greatest command, the Spirit of God is making us a bride: a people who are wholly consumed with love for her Bridegroom.

Like the Early Church, all these dimensions of our corporate identity are outworked through a vast network of small groups. These groups are spread all throughout the nations and are connected by golden threads—unbreakable relationships which have been woven in the love of God. This love unites the entire net so that when one person or a group has a need, the whole network of families can come together to meet that need. This is God's design and He is making it a reality. Will you join Him?

Group Structures

10

In many ways, Christianity is like basketball. We might fall in love with the game, learn the rules, and practice all the different skills needed to play basketball. We might even become the best shooter in the world. But we will never begin to play basketball until we join a team, get on court and start to play the game. While individual practice is important, basketball will always be a team sport.

In the same way, we may hear the gospel, fall in love with Jesus and then go home and pray to God and worship Him. We might study the Bible and even become the most famous theologian in the world. But we won't be truly following Jesus until we join with other believers and begin to love one another. This is Christ's new command and so this is where we must start.

As we begin, we need to remember that love flows the strongest in the smallest numbers, and so the small family groups must be our highest priority. But what do these small groups look like? How big are they? And what do they do when they meet together?

There is only so much time in the day, and so we are naturally limited in the number of close relationships we can have. Jesus had an inner group of three (His team of Peter, James and John) who received most of His time, and then the 12 disciples (His family), then a larger group of 70 or more followers (His close network). John Wesley followed this model and organized people into similarly sized groups in the Great Awakening. At the foundation were teams of three or four that he called *bands*. Larger groups of 12-20 were called *classes* and these classes combined to form groups of 70 or more that were called *societies*. At every level, these groups had an unwavering focus on loving God and loving one another, which led England into her first great awakening.

Teams

In our fellowship, we call our smallest groups, *teams*. These are groups of between two and four people who are devoted to living in God's design of love. The goal of these groups is to:

-Spur each other on to love, which involves:

- encouraging each other to greater depths of intimacy and unity with Jesus,
- being accountable to the commands of love,
- praying for healing, energizing, and empowerment,
- investing in each other's lives.

- Live in the light with one another, which involves:

- sharing real testimonies of our spiritual journey,
- confessing any sin,
- sharing victories over temptation,
- honestly expressing our heart to one another.

People can be a part of more than one team, and teams can meet in person or online. There is no set structure for these meetings. Some teams spend the time sharing and praying for one another. Others focus on going deep into the Scriptures. Some meet to eat together while they discuss their spiritual growth. Some share testimonies. Some work through the Bible or a book in their own time and then come together to share their insights and experiences. All seek to spur each other on to love.

In terms of accountability, there are small groups that use a 0-10 scale to share where they are in terms of their physical, emotional, relational and spiritual health. This can be useful to quickly identify the areas that people need help or encouragement in. Some teams have a set of probing questions that are drawn out at random, and people answer as honestly as they can. Example questions can be found at onewithchrist.org/teamquestions

Spiritual Family Groups

1 Corinthians 14:26

What then, brothers? When you come together, each one has a hymn, a lesson, a revelation, a tongue, or an interpretation. Let all things be done for building up.

The Early Church called their larger family meetings "love feasts."[45] These gatherings were celebrations in which everyone shared food, ministry and conversation. Each person was valued for who God created them to be and for the unique blessings they brought to the group.

Family meetings can take place weekly, fortnightly or even monthly. In our family meetings, we seek to make sure that everyone participates in the flow of love and so we encourage everyone to come with something to give. It may be an uplifting or prophetic word to share one-on-one with a person or it may be a teaching for the whole group. One day, someone may give a testimony to inspire three or four others. On a different day, they may feel led to pray for a person, minister in their spiritual gifts or give someone else an actual gift. The Spirit-led nature of the love means that each meeting has a wonderful sense of unpredictability about it. It also means that each person leaves feeling valued and enriched.

Because love is the overarching goal of these meetings, we make plenty of time for people to connect with one another. The conversations that take place over food allow people to be known and loved. As people listen, encourage, pray for and minister to one another, the golden threads are woven in a way that delights the heart of God.

Special Focus Groups

These groups are formed for a specific purpose and season. They are usually based around a gifting or ministry and can be used to develop maturity in a specific area of spiritual life. For example, the Lord may lead someone to begin a Bible study group. Those who feel led to participate can then join in. These special focus groups help people to grow in their calling by giving them the opportunity to practice using their gifts. These groups can be many and varied and may run just for a season or indefinitely. The focus of such groups may include:

- exploring the gospel with new or non-believers
- praise and worship
- prayer ministry and growing in spiritual gifts
- missions support and development
- teaching and Bible study
- community ministry and more

Unique Glory of Unique Cultures

The way people live as families across the world varies with culture, yet the fundamental design of family is universal. This is also true spiritually. As a network of spiritual families, we all have different cultural backgrounds which will shape the style and beauty of our group. The food we eat, the nature of our conversation, how we read the word of God, the way we honor one another, the kind of praise and the style of ministry; these will all be influenced by our culture. And these differences (insofar as they are holy) are to be celebrated. Knowing this, there is no exact formula for how a meeting should look, except that the love of God should be on full display. It is this love for Jesus and for one another that transcends our cultural differences and unites us all as one family in Christ.

Unity

11

In our journey to becoming one in Christ, it can be helpful to learn how people in the past overcame divisions and managed to cultivate a lasting sense of unity. One such man was Nicolaus Ludwig (Count of Zinzendorf), who in 1722 allowed Protestant refugees to settle on his land in Hernnhut Germany. These refugees came from different backgrounds and held differing beliefs which at times enriched the community and at other times created significant conflict.

Ludwig wanted to find a way for people to live together in peace and unity. He met with individuals and groups in the community and together they prayed and searched the Scriptures for an answer to the conflict. The answer they found was profound and life-changing: *love one another.* The people took the new command seriously and started to meet in small groups and to foster a sense of spiritual family. They agreed upon a code of life which was based largely on the Moravian principle of:

"In essentials unity, in non-essentials liberty, and in all things love."

Within the community, this simple phrase brought unity by helping people to keep the design of love as their main focus. It created space for people to have differing perspectives on minor topics without letting their opinions compromise the flow of love. The first command was put into first place, and like a golden thread, God's love wove from heart to heart and united the people as a true spiritual family.

If we are to follow a similar pattern, the following statements of belief may be helpful as a list of essentials to unite small groups in the net:

- We believe that the God of the Bible is the eternal Creator who made all things.
- Jesus is the Word who is both with God and is God. He is the uncreated Son of God, eternally one with the Father.
- God gives us the Holy Spirit to live within us and unite us with the Father and the Son.
- We believe that the Scriptures are true, and that Jesus became human, lived among us, and then died upon the cross to take away our sin and selfishness.
- We believe that Jesus was raised to life on the third day and that He ascended into heaven and is returning in glory and power.
- We believe that Jesus died not only to get us into heaven, but to restore our design of love. We believe that anyone can receive God's forgiveness, be filled with His Spirit, and enter a life of love through the gift of God's grace.
- Because grace is a gift, we can only receive it through faith. Faith is the confidence of the heart that trusts in God and accepts His blessings without trying to earn them.
- We believe that the greatest command is the ultimate call for every believer and that in unity with Jesus, we can love God with all our heart, soul, mind and strength.
- We believe that our faith is primarily expressed not by what we say we believe, but by our love for one another. Jesus gave us the new commandment and if we are willing, He will help us to love one another as He loves us.

An Invitation

If you want to pursue a life of loving God and loving others, we would like to invite you to gather two or three people and create a team. Encourage others to start their own team and then bring those teams together and forge a spiritual family. Eat together and get to really know each other. Pray for one another, minister and spur each other on to love. Meet needs and orchestrate joy. Then connect with other people in other groups. Let your hearts be woven together by God into an unbreakable net. Grow. Be fruitful. Flourish and multiply!

If you would like to link with other small groups in your area, we have a website that allows leaders to connect, share needs, impart wisdom, and pass on their experiences. It includes a knowledge base that gives Biblical guidance on common issues that arise in small groups as well as a digital mentoring platform to support people as they grow. These are all available for free at **oneanother.net** or you can email us at **info@oneanother.net**

Additional Resources

Hebrews 6:1 (NASB)
Therefore leaving the elementary teaching about the Christ, let us press on to maturity,

Scripture calls us to pursue maturity, and this must be a daily pursuit. To this end, many small groups read the Bible or work through books at home and then share their revelations and insights when they come together. Working through Biblical material at home is a valuable way of sustaining spiritual growth between meetings.

It is important to remember the design of love when selecting reading material for a group. If a resource does not help us to love God more or love each other more, it is either a distraction or a deception. Therefore, we must let the Lord lead us and do our best to keep the greatest commands in focus.

To help get started, the following material affirms the design of love and is available free online at **onewithchrist.org**

- **One with Christ Series**
  These books take readers on a journey into the love of God. *First Love* is about the design of life; *Bride Arise* is about experiencing Jesus as our Bridegroom; *And He Will* is about the power of the cross to bring us into covenant love.

- **Five More Minutes**
  This is a small book that explores the design of love and the power of small groups to change the world.

- **Discover Jesus**
  This is a 12-week course for new believers and enquirers.

- **Follow Me**
  This is a 45-week Bible study series for foundations in the faith.

- **Flowers and Prickles**
  This is a guided conversation for children to help them process hurt and connect with Jesus in a living and real way.

- **Valuable**
  This is a small book that is written for non-believers and new Christians. It explores the design of love from philosophical, scientific, social, and spiritual angles. It challenges the reader to open their hearts to consider Jesus Christ and His message of love.

Please visit **onewithchrist.org** for these and other resources, including these additional chapters of *Golden Threads*: Church as a House of Prayer, Church as an Ecclesia, and Women in the Church.

Questions and Objections

Finally, join us at **oneanother.net** to explore questions like these:

- Can we be a part of a net and belong to a traditional large-scale church?
- Is there still a place for the big service?
- Is it enough to belong to a house-church style fellowship or do Christians need to also belong to a denominational church to be spiritually safe?
- I don't know how to teach and don't feel qualified to start a group. Where do I start?
- I already have a home fellowship, but we'd like to connect to other groups in our area. How do we do that?
- If I start a team or small group, whose authority will I be under?
- What does accountability look like in small groups?
- How can I be sure that I won't be deceived like so many small groups have been in the past?
- Can we use titles like *Pastor* or *Apostle* in a small group?
- Are women allowed to speak in a homegroup?
- Do we need to tithe in small groups?

If you have other questions you would like to explore, please connect with us at **oneanother.net**

Final Prayer

Thank you for taking the time to read this short book. I hope that you have been inspired to pursue God's vision for your life both individually and with other believers. If you would like to receive more regular content, please connect with us online.

Now, may the God of all glory, the Father of lights, our great King of eternity saturate your life with His presence. May He settle you in a family and flood your life with His love from every direction. May the Father share the depths of His love for Jesus with you. May you have eyes to see Jesus and to behold His unfading beauty. May you establish a throne in your heart for Christ by making a covenant to love God with all your heart, soul, mind and strength, and to love Jesus through His people. May His love flow through you like a river of fire. May you know the fullness of joy, a life of abundance, a love without measure, and the peace of Christ that transcends all understanding. May you fall ever deeper in love with Jesus and come to know Him as your bridegroom king. May you rest in His covenant love for you that Scripture says stretches from eternity to eternity. And may you be one with Christ forever.

- *Geoff Woodcock, Author*

onewithchrist.org | oneanother.net

Get More Resources

The **onewithchrist.org** website also contains other books and resources available free to download, including the One with Christ series of books.

Connect with Us

Visit **oneanother.net** to connect with other spiritual family groups.

oneanother.net

Purchase Artwork

Visit **mariakemp.art** to purchase prints of the Golden Threads cover art.

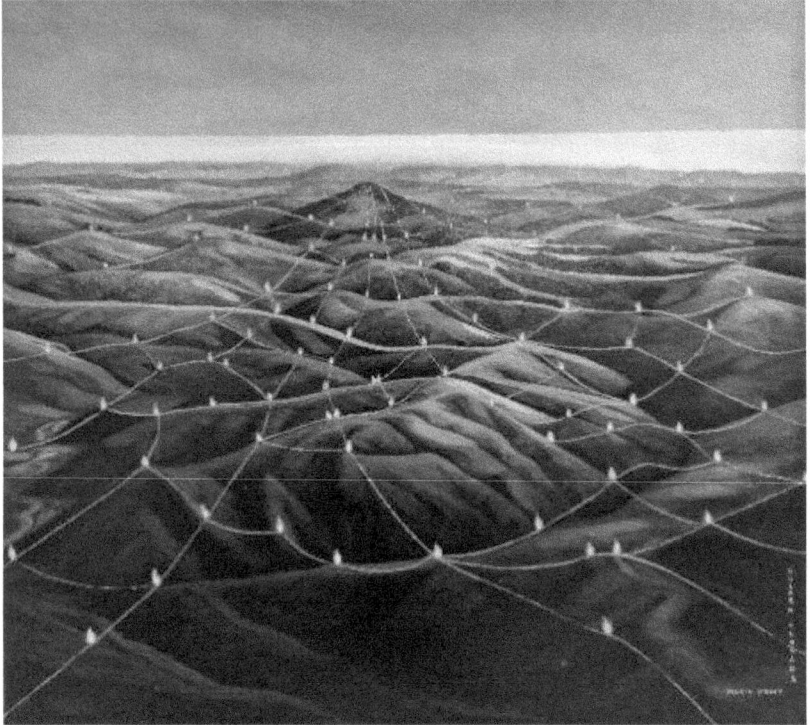

References

[1] Isaiah 61:1, John 15:11

[2] Matthew 11:28-29, Philippians 4:7

[3] Psalm 103:8-12, John 8:31-32

[4] Psalm 103:17

[5] In Psalm 23:6, the imperfect tense is used for the word *radaph,* which is translated as *follow,* but more accurately means to *chase or pursue.* The imperfect tense signifies an ongoing or continuous action.

[6] Jeremiah 33:9

[7] Psalm 119:68

[8] See Colossians 1:15-16. God created everything through Jesus and for Jesus, including us.

[9] Genesis 1:31

[10] Can any mind comprehend an infinite, eternal creator God who is the perfection of goodness, the defining Source of all that is pure and true? Even if we go to the very limits of our imagination, we will still not be able to capture the slightest fraction of the nature of God. If God is good beyond all comprehension, then it stands to reason that His vision for us must likewise be better than anything we can imagine. From this perspective, if something appears "too good to be true," we need to reframe it as "so unbelievably good that it can only be God."

[11] See Deuteronomy 30:6-14. We look at the greatest command in more detail in the *One with Christ* books, available free at onewithchrist.org

[12] See Romans 5:2—wholehearted love is a gift of grace that we only access by faith.

[13] 1 Corinthians 6:17

[14] John 8:31-32, Romans 8:37

[15] John 10:10, John 17:20-26

[16] Psalm 16:11

[17] Isaiah 9:6

[18] 2 Corinthians 3:17, Colossians 2:13-15

[19] 1 John 5:11-12, 20

[20] Hebrews 1:3

[21] 1 John 5:3

²² As valuable as our worship songs are, if we spend more time singing to God than loving one another then our lives are out of balance with His design.

²³ 2 Corinthians 1:3-4. God comforts us so that we might be able to comfort others. He blesses us so that we might be able to share that blessing with other people.

²⁴ 2 Corinthians 5:14-15

²⁵ Matthew 6:25-33

²⁶ This quotation is taken from the NASB 1995 edition, with the words "from a pure" added (as *pure* is present in the original Greek but left untranslated in the NASB.)

²⁷ The word *brethren* literally means *brothers,* however like our English word *guys,* it is most often used to refer to a related mixed group of both men and women. Therefore, when we read the word *brethren,* we can simply think *family.*

²⁸ Psalm 16:3

²⁹ Acts 3:1-26; 5:20, 42

³⁰ Quoted in *The Good and Beautiful Community : Following the Spirit, Extending Grace, Demonstrating Love* by James Bryan Smith, InterVarsity Press.

³¹ Galatians 5:4

³² Elwell, Walter A. *Evangelical Dictionary of Biblical Theology.* Grand Rapids, Mich: Baker Books, 1996; *Sanctification*

³³ 1 John 1:9

³⁴ See https://oneanother.net/women-in-ministry

³⁵ To learn more of our value to God, read Chapters 2-4 of *Bride Arise* available at onewithchrist.org

³⁶ Luke 5:34-35, Matthew 22:1-14, Revelation 21:1-4

³⁷ If the language of marriage is a barrier, feel free to drop the terms of bride and Bridegroom and simply focus on making a covenant of love with Jesus.

³⁸ John 17:26

³⁹ Acts 4.32

⁴⁰ To explore this more, get *Five more Minutes,* available at onewithchrist.org

⁴¹ Acts 11:27-30

⁴² 2 Thessalonians 3:10

⁴³ Ephesians 4:28

⁴⁴ Acts 13:1-3

⁴⁵ Jude 1:12

www.ingramcontent.com/pod-product-compliance
Lightning Source LLC
Chambersburg PA
CBHW071847020426
42331CB00007B/1888

* 9 7 8 1 9 9 1 3 8 7 3 8 7 *